Myths and Tales

Greta Speechley

WAYLAND

This edition published in 2007 by Wayland

Wayland
338 Euston Road
London NW1 3BH

Wayland Australia
Hachette Children's Books
Level 17/207 Kent Street
Sydney, NSW 2000

For The Brown Reference Group plc.
Craftperson: Greta Speechley
Project Editor: Jane Scarsbrook
Designer: Joan Curtis
Photography: Martin Norris
Design Manager: Lynne Ross
Managing Editor: Bridget Giles
Editorial Director: Lindsey Lowe

British Library Cataloguing in Publication Data

Speechley, Greta, 1948-
   Myths & tales. - (Crafts for kids)
   1. Handicraft - Juvenile literature 2. Myth in art - Juvenile
   literature 3. Legends in art - Juvenile literature
   I. Title
   745.5'9

ISBN-13: 9780750251563

ISBN: 978-0-7502-5156-3

Printed and bound in Thailand

Wayland is a division of Hachette Children's Books

Contents

Introduction

Myths are exciting stories with fantastical creatures and characters. Every country has a wealth of tales for you to learn about and this book is full of craft projects inspired by some of the most magical stories. There is a Trojan horse toy box from an old Greek myth, and there are mischievous pixies and flitting fairies to make.

YOU WILL NEED

Each project includes a list of all the things you need. Before you buy new materials, look at home to see what you could use instead. For example, you can cut any card shapes out of an empty cereal box. You can buy other items, such as air-drying clay and felt from a craft shop. You can buy silver sand for the Sand painting from a garden centre. For the Flying fairies you will need to buy pink kitchen scourers from a supermarket.

Getting started

 Read the steps for the project first.

 Gather together all the items you need.

 Cover your work surface with newspaper.

 Wear an apron or change into old clothes.

A message for adults

All the projects in Myths and Tales have been designed for children to make, but occasionally they will need you to help. Some of the projects do require the use of sharp utensils, such as scissors or needles. Please read the instructions before your child starts work.

Making patterns

Follow these steps to make the patterns on pages 30 and 31. Using a pencil, trace the pattern on to tracing paper. If you're making a project out of fabric, you can cut out the tracing paper pattern and pin it on to the fabric. To cut the pattern out of card, turn the tracing over and lay it on to the card. Rub firmly over the pattern with a pencil. The shape will appear on the card. Cut out the shape.

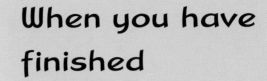

When you have finished

 Wash paintbrushes and put everything away.

 Put pens, pencils, paints and glue in an old box or ice cream container.

 Keep scissors and other sharp items in a safe place.

 Stick needles and pins into a pincushion or a piece of scrap cloth.

BE SAFE

Look out for the safety boxes. They will appear whenever you need to ask an adult for help.

Ask an adult to help you use sharp scissors.

Magic amulet

In many tales the hero or heroine has a magic amulet with special powers. Make your own amulet and see if it brings you good luck.

YOU WILL NEED

white plastic drink bottle	purple foil sweet wrappers
marker pen	silver spray paint
scissors	hole punch
gold and purple thin tinsel	black cord
small, round candle base	plastic bag tie
shiny bobble	needle
	glue

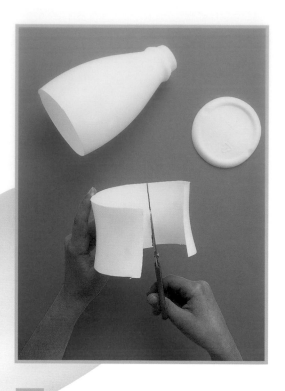

1 Mark off a section on the plastic drink bottle that is about 7.5 cm (3 in) tall and goes about halfway around the bottle. Cut it out.

2 Punch holes along the sides of the armband using a hole punch and make two holes at either end. Spray the band silver.

6

3 Thread thin tinsel along the edges. Make two holes in the base of the candle case and in the middle of the armband using a needle. Push a plastic bag tie through both pieces and twist the ends.

4 Glue purple tinsel on to the amulet around the candle case. Wind gold tinsel into a coil and glue it inside the candle holder.

5 Glue a shiny purple bobble to the centre. Scrunch purple foil wrappers into balls and glue them to the amulet on either side of the centrepiece. Thread two black cords through the holes in the amulet so you can tie it around your arm.

Snake demon

This fierce snake demon from Sri Lanka is said to frighten away evil spirits. The hissing snakes are made from twisted newspaper covered with papier mâché.

YOU WILL NEED

newspaper	tissue paper
card	PVA glue
scissors	mixing bowl
pencil	poster paints
tape	paintbrush

1 Draw the demon's face on to the card. Draw three wiggly snakes at the top for hair and two large nostrils in the middle. Cut out the demon drawing.

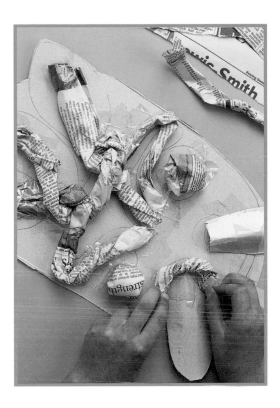

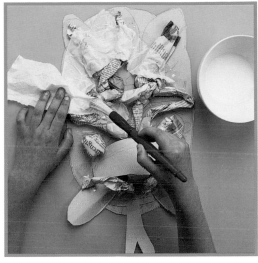

2 Cut two snake heads out of cardboard and tape them to the face so they are coming out of the nostrils! Tape on a forked tongue at the bottom, too. Twist newspaper and tape it over the lines you have drawn for the snake hair and the nostrils. Tape on balls of newspaper for eyes.

3 To make a nose, cut a piece of card that fits around the nostrils. Tape it in place.

4 Mix up half PVA glue and half water in a bowl. Tear up strips of tissue paper and paste them all over the snake demon. Let each layer dry and paste on three layers in total.

5 Have fun painting your snake demon and then hang it up on your door to keep out pests!

Little lyre

One Greek myth tells how the god Hermes invented the lyre. He scooped out a tortoise and used the shell as a musical instrument to charm the other gods. Make a lyre from paper plates and charm everyone by singing along as you strum!

YOU WILL NEED

four paper plates	tape
pencil	short piece of bamboo or dowel
scissors	
felt-tip pens	small plastic beads
wooden skewer	scissors
black wool	glue

1 Cut two horseshoe shapes out of two paper plates. They make the arms of the lyre.

2 Cut a curved piece out of a third paper plate. Do this by drawing around the edge of one of the arm pieces. It makes one side of the body of the lyre.

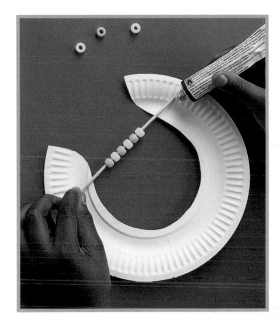

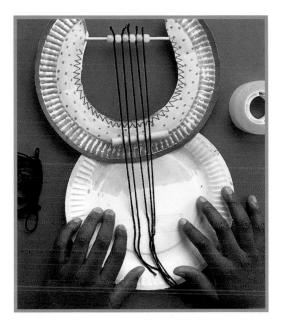

3 Colour in the pieces. Take a fourth plate and decorate it in a tortoiseshell pattern. It is the other side of the body of the lyre.

4 Thread six beads on to a wooden skewer. Glue the skewer to the back of one of the arm pieces. Glue the second arm piece on top.

5 Glue the arms to the inside of the tortoiseshell piece. Colour in the inside as shown because this part will show. Glue a short piece of bamboo to the bottom of the arms for the strings to rest on. To make the strings, tie lengths of wool between each bead and tape them in place further down.

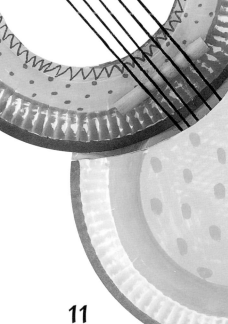

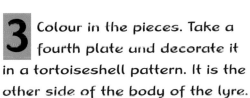

6 Glue the last piece over the strings as shown.

Sand painting

The Navajo people from Southwest USA are famous for making spectacular sand paintings on the ground. In Navajo healing ceremonies a sick person sits on the sand picture and then the sand is rubbed over his or her body.

YOU WILL NEED

silver sand (sandpit sand)	scrap cardboard
mixing bowl	white card
mixing stick	glue
poster paints	paintbrush
pestle and mortar or a stone	wooden picture frame
pencil	scissors
	cord

1 Mix up sand with a little paint. Spread out the sand on cardboard to dry. Crush any lumps in the sand with a stone. You could use a pestle and mortar to grind the sand smooth if you have one. Make four or five colours of sand.

12

2 Cut out a rectangle of white card to fit in your wooden frame. Draw on a design using a pencil.

3 Paint glue on to the area you want to colour, then sprinkle on coloured sand. To make the rocket picture on the opposite page, we sprinkled on glitter as well.

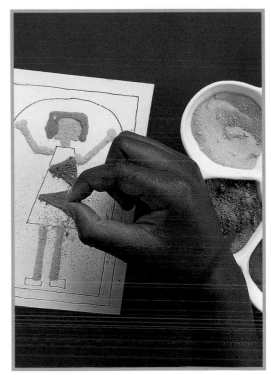

4 Shake off the extra sand and glue another area. Sprinkle on a different colour of sand.

5 Let the glue dry and then fit the picture into the back of the frame. Press down the tabs on the back of the frame to keep the picture in place.

Glinting dagger

Every hero or heroine needs a
weapon to fight off mythical beasts.
Decorate this dagger with a glittering
hilt (handle), then make up an
adventurous myth starring you
as the brave hero.

YOU WILL NEED

strong cardboard	scissors
tracing paper	glitter pens in different colours
pencil	colours
ruler	kitchen foil
glue	

1 Trace the dagger pattern on page 30 using a
ruler to make the straight lines. Transfer the
tracing on to strong cardboard following the
instructions on page 5. Cut out the cardboard dagger.

14

2 Cover the blade with kitchen foil, and stick it down with glue. Smooth the foil surface with your thumbs to get rid of wrinkles.

3 Decorate the hilt with glitter pens. We have drawn on an outline with green glitter and added a fan pattern with purple glitter.

4 Fill in the pattern and background using different-coloured glitter pens. Let one side dry thoroughly before decorating the other.

Pixie pen tops

Pixies are tiny characters from English folk stories. They love playing tricks such as pointing travellers in the wrong direction and blowing out candles!

YOU WILL NEED

air-drying clay	thin paintbrush
pencil	varnish
poster paints	clay cutter

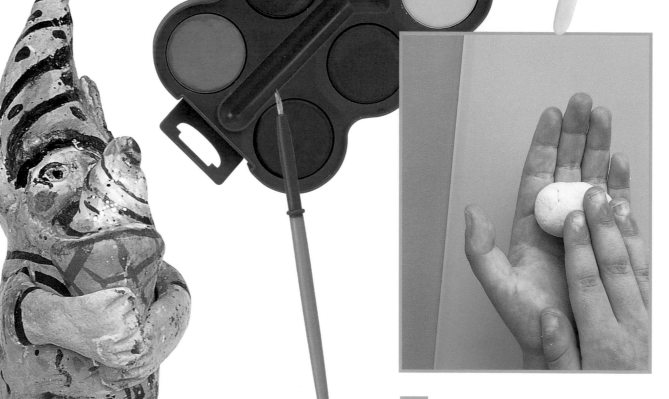

1 Take a chunk of clay and roll it into a short, fat sausage.

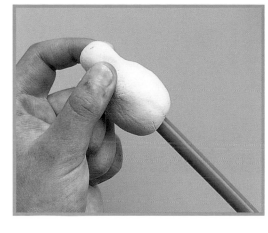

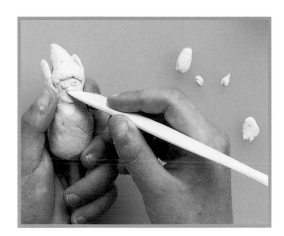

2 Push the end of a pencil into the chunk of clay.

3 Shape the clay into a body with a head by squeezing it with your fingers.

4 Make a pointy pixie hat and pointy ears from clay. Press them on to the pixie's head. Press on tiny balls of clay for eyes, a nose and a mouth.

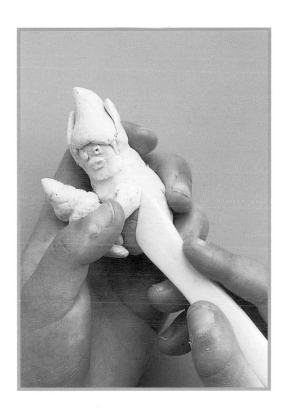

5 Our pixie has stolen an ice cream! Make an ice cream cone from clay and two sausages for arms. Press them on to the pixie with the arms folding around the cone. You can use a modelling tool such as a clay cutter to add detail to your pixie's clothes.

6 Take the pixie off the pencil and let the clay dry and harden. Paint the pixie with lots of bright colours. You will need a very thin paintbrush. Let the paint dry. Paint the pixie with a layer of varnish to give it a shiny finish.

Pot of gold

Have you heard the tale that at the end of every rainbow there is a pot of gold? This is a charming golden money box with a rainbow chute to slide your coins down.

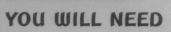

YOU WILL NEED

thin card	gold paper
tracing paper	glue
pencil	felt in different
scissors	colours
round yogurt	poster paints
container	paintbrush
box	paper

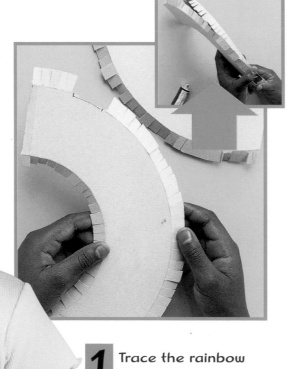

1 Trace the rainbow pattern on page 31. Transfer the shape on to card following the instructions on page 5. Do this twice and cut out the two shapes. Glue the pieces together using the tabs. The coin slots must be together.

2 Paint a rainbow on to white paper using a watery brush. Make it slightly bigger than the card rainbow. Glue it on to the card rainbow chute.

18

3 Choose a box and cut a slot in the side of it for the rainbow to fit into. Paint a wash of blue on to white card to make a sky background. Glue it to the back of the box. Glue the rainbow chute to the sky with its end over the slot in the box.

4 Cut the bottom out of a yogurt container and cut out a section from the side. It is the pot of gold. Cover it in gold paper and fit it around the bottom of the rainbow. Glue it in place.

5 Cover the box with green felt. Make a spiky fringe at the top to look like grass. Cut out felt flowers and glue them on. Glue a white paper cloud to the sky, too.

19

Phoenix clip

The ancient Egyptians told stories about a fabulous bird called the phoenix. They said it had scarlet and gold feathers and lived for about 500 years! Add a clip and a magnet to your phoenix so it can hold notes and lists in its beak.

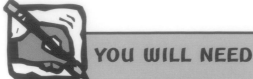

YOU WILL NEED

tracing paper
pencil
gold paper
felt in different colours
six flexible straws
tape
card
gold and silver glitter pens
glue
magnet
clothes clip
feathers from a clothes shop
scissors

1 Trace the phoenix on page 31. Transfer the tracing on to card, following the instructions on page 5. Cut out the shape. Trace the bird again on to a separate piece of card. This time, cut out the beak, head and leg shapes separately. Use the pieces as templates to cut out a beak from gold paper, a red felt body, a pink felt head and blue felt legs. Cut the felt slightly bigger than the templates.

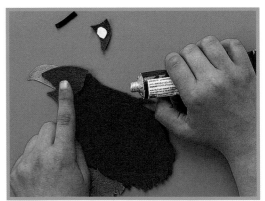

2 Feather the felt edges by making small snips with the scissors. Glue the pieces on to the card bird. Cut out an eye from purple felt and a white felt iris and black pupil. Glue them on.

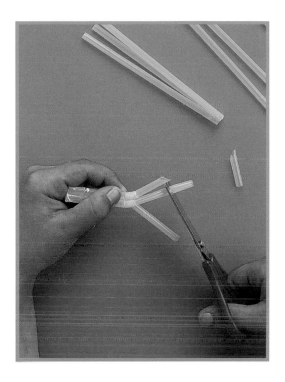

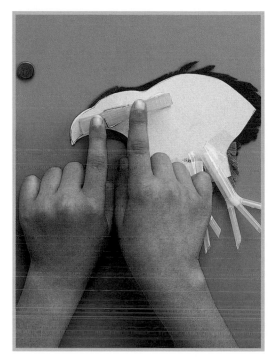

3 To make a foot, tape three flexible straws together just above the bend. Cut them to size and cut the feet at an angle to make pointy claws. Make a second foot and tape them to the back of the bird's legs.

4 Glue a clothes clip to the back of the bird, with the clamping end near the beak. Glue a magnet to the clip.

5 Decorate the bird with dots of glitter. Glue feathers to the tail and the top of the head. Your phoenix can hold a note in its beak. You can attach it to the door of the fridge.

Cyclops eye

A cyclops is a giant with one eye in the middle of his forehead. In Greek myths, the cyclops giants make thunderbolts for the god Zeus, and the giants also gobble up people!

Ask an adult to read step 1 and make the paper pulp.

YOU WILL NEED

small egg carton	PVA glue
saucepan	jar lid
food processor	clay cutter
stirring spoon	poster paints
bowl	paintbrush
	clear glue
	brooch back

1 Tear up the egg crate into pieces and put them in a bowl. Cover them with water and let them soak for a couple of days. Ask an adult to boil the mixture in a saucepan for about 20 minutes and then smash it up into a pulp in a food processor. Pour the pulp into a sieve and squeeze out most of the water.

2 Put the pulp into a bowl and add a big blob of PVA glue. Stir it up to make a sticky pulp.

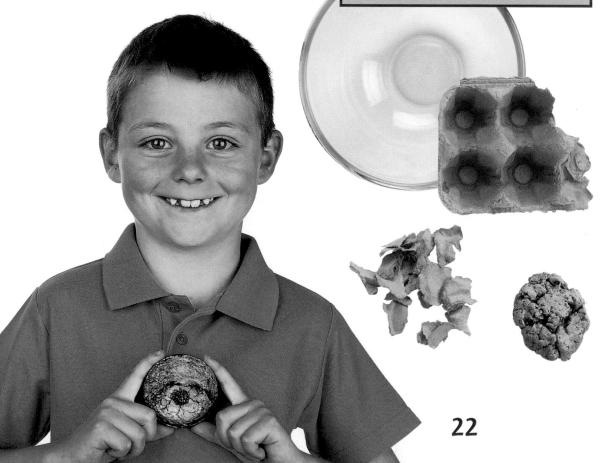

22

3 Use a clay cutter to press a layer of pulp into the jar lid.

4 To make the pupil, roll up a ball of pulp and press it on. Shape an eyelid from the pulp and press it on to the rim of the jar lid. Let the eye dry thoroughly.

5 Paint the pulp eye in gruesome colours. Let the paint dry.

6 Glue a brooch pin to the back of the jar lid so you can wear the eye as a badge.

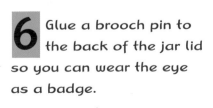

Totem pole

In Northwest USA, the Tlingit people carve logs to make totem poles. The characters on a totem pole are often animals and mythical creatures. Make your own totem pole with unusual animal faces.

Ask an adult to check that the tin cans have no sharp edges

YOU WILL NEED

three tin cans	poster paints
paper bowl	paintbrush
card	tissue paper
tape	PVA glue
scissors	mixing bowl
glue	egg carton

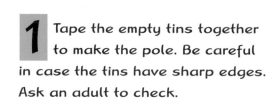

1 Tape the empty tins together to make the pole. Be careful in case the tins have sharp edges. Ask an adult to check.

2 Cut the paper bowl in half and glue the two pieces together to make the head crest. Cut an egg carton to make noses and beaks for your characters.

24

3 Tape the head crest to the top of the pole.

4 Tape on the egg-carton beaks and cut out two wings from card. Tape them to the sides of the totem pole. Scrunch up tissue paper into balls and tape them to the pole to make eyes for the creatures.

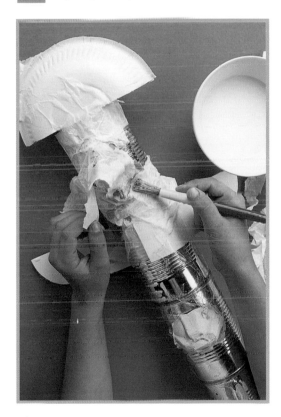

5 Mix up half PVA glue and half water in a bowl. Tear up strips of tissue paper and paste them all over the totem pole. Let each layer dry and paste on two or three layers in all.

6 Paint the totem pole in bright colours, one animal on top of another.

Trojan horse

A famous legend tells how the Greeks gave a huge wooden horse as a gift to the city of Troy. When the people of Troy were asleep, Greek soldiers leaped out of the horse and overtook the city! Make a horse of your own as a toy box.

1 To make the legs, cut a fringe around the top and bottom of four toilet paper tubes. Bend back the tabs. Cover the legs with orange felt.

2 Cover the box and the juice carton with orange felt to make the head and body. Make a lift-up lid for the body by cutting along three sides at the top, but leaving one side in place. Glue to the head a mouth cut from white felt. Draw on teeth with a pen.

YOU WILL NEED

large box for the body
small juice carton for the head
orange, black and white felt
scissors
pen
glue

four toilet paper tubes
cork
scissors
strong cardboard for the base
two wooden skewers

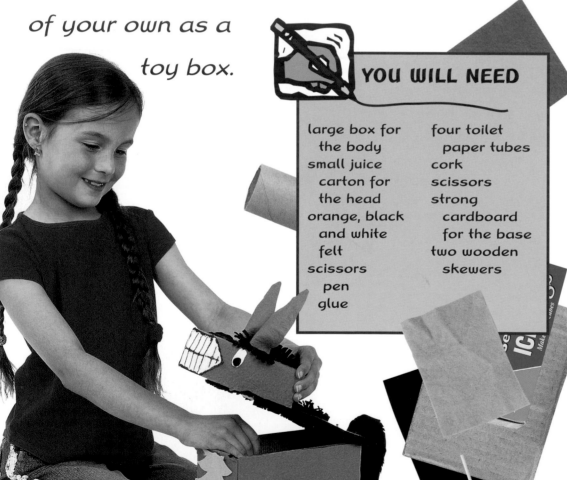

26

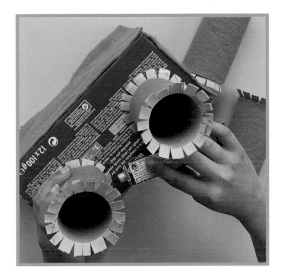

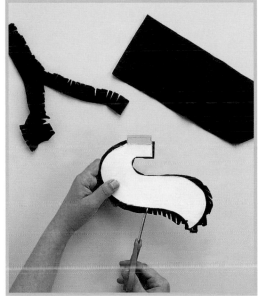

3 Glue the legs to the bottom of the body using the tabs. Glue the head to the lid flap on the top of the body.

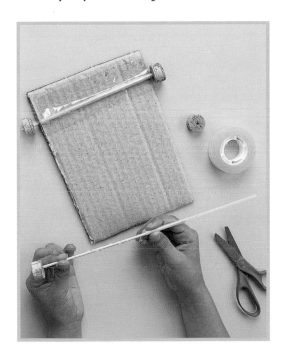

4 Trace the tail shape on page 30. Transfer the tracing on to cardboard following the instructions on page 5. Cut out the cardboard tail. Cut two pieces of black felt slightly bigger than the tail. Do this by drawing around the cardboard. Glue them to either side of the tail and cut a fringe around the edge.

5 Glue the tail to the back of the body using the tab. Cut a fringe of black felt to go around the horse's body and head. Cut out ears from orange felt and eyes from white and black felt. Glue them to the horse's head.

6 To make the base, tape two skewers to a piece of strong cardboard. Push slices of cork on to the ends of the skewers as wheels. Ask an adult to cut the cork for you. Now glue the horse on top using the tabs on the legs.

Ask an adult to cut a cork to make the wheels.

Flying fairies

Fairies are tiny magical creatures that appear in stories all over the world. They are pretty and charming and these have lovely pink skirts made from kitchen scourers! Make a few fairies to hang from a flowery mobile in your bedroom.

YOU WILL NEED

round, pink kitchen scourer
four wooden beads for heads
multi-coloured wool for hair
golden wire for the bodies
small beads for hands and feet
thread
dried moss
green tinsel
fabric flowers
butterfly hair clips

1 To make the first fairy, cut a snip in the centre of a scourer. Cut off a layer of scourer to make a fairy skirt.

2 Bend a piece of golden wire in half to make two long legs and push it through the centre of the skirt. Wind golden wire around the middle to keep the skirt and legs in place. Leave two ends sticking out to be the arms.

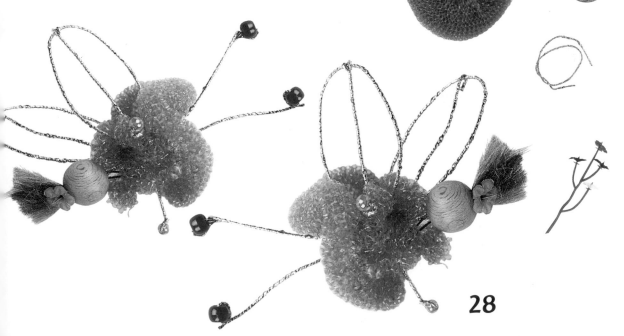

28

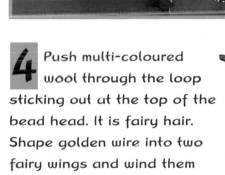

3 Thread beads on to the ends of the legs and arms to make feet and hands. Thread a big wooden bead on to the loop of wire at the top to make the fairy's head.

4 Push multi-coloured wool through the loop sticking out at the top of the bead head. It is fairy hair. Shape golden wire into two fairy wings and wind them around the fairy's body. Make three fairies in this way.

5 To make the flower ring, make a ring from wire, leaving plenty of wire at the end. Press dried moss around the ring and wind the spare wire around to keep the grass in place. Wind green tinsel around the ring and push in fabric flowers. Add butterfly hair clips, too. Wind on three lengths of wire so you can hang up the mobile. Tie the fairies to the ring with thin thread.

Patterns

Here are the patterns you will need to make some of the projects. To find out how to make a pattern, follow the instructions in the "Making patterns" box on page 5. Sometimes you will need to cut out two shapes using the same tracing. This is indicated on the pattern.

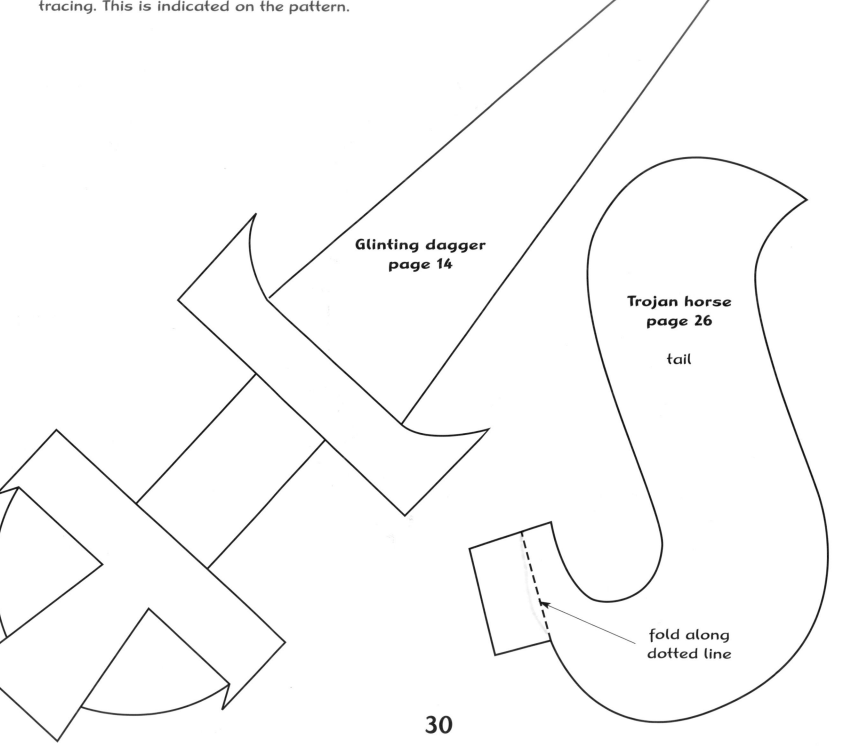

**Glinting dagger
page 14**

**Trojan horse
page 26**

tail

fold along
dotted line

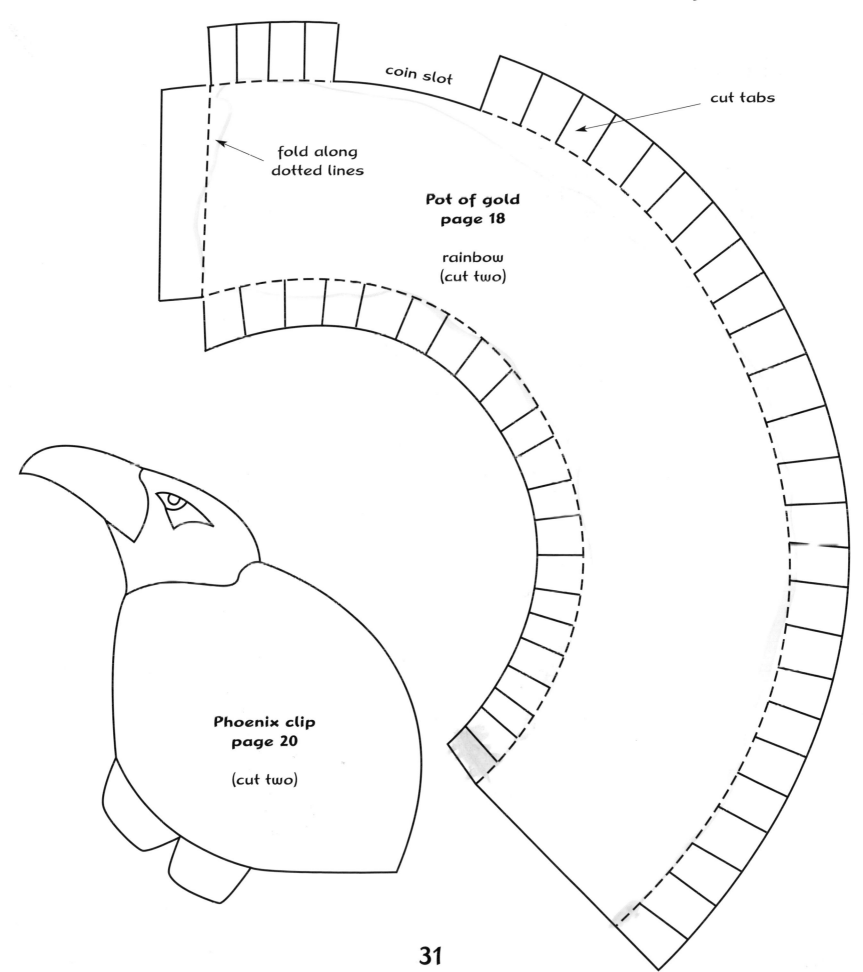

coin slot

cut tabs

fold along
dotted lines

**Pot of gold
page 18**

rainbow
(cut two)

**Phoenix clip
page 20**

(cut two)

Index

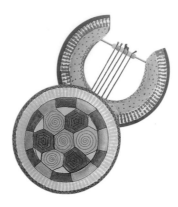